RANDALL HARTSELL

FOREWORD

A vacation spot, special movie or favorite book viewed through the eyes of a child takes on a totally new appearance when viewed with the eyes of an adult. Our life experiences, education and wisdom give us new insights into past experiences and familiar places. The hymns in this book were conceived with this idea in mind.

The subtle changes in melodic lines and surprising harmonic turns are designed to add new life to some of our favorite hymns. Although these arrangements may be successfully used to stimulate interest in piano study or enrich a worship service, they were also composed to bring renewed energy and insight to the performance of familiar hymns.

Best wishes as you see through new eyes!

CONTENTS

Cover photo: Leland Howard

Fairest Lord Jesus

Silesian Folk Tune
Arranged by Randall Hartsell

My Faith Looks Up to Thee

Lowell Mason
Arranged by Randall Hartsell

5

For the Beauty of the Earth

Conrad Kocher
Arranged by Randall Hartsell

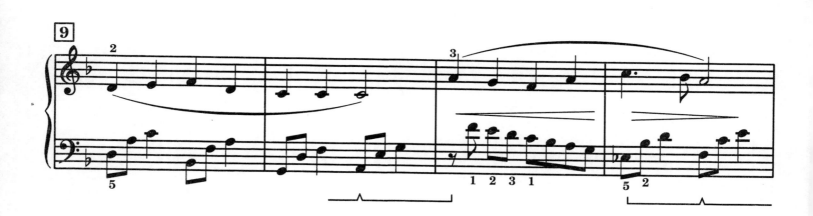

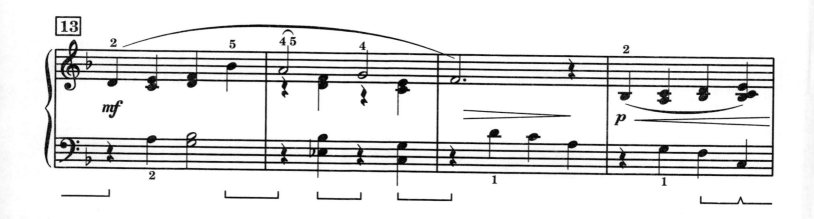

This Is My Father's World

Franklin L. Sheppard
Arranged by Randall Hartsell

9

A Mighty Fortress Is Our God

Martin Luther
Arranged by Randall Hartsell

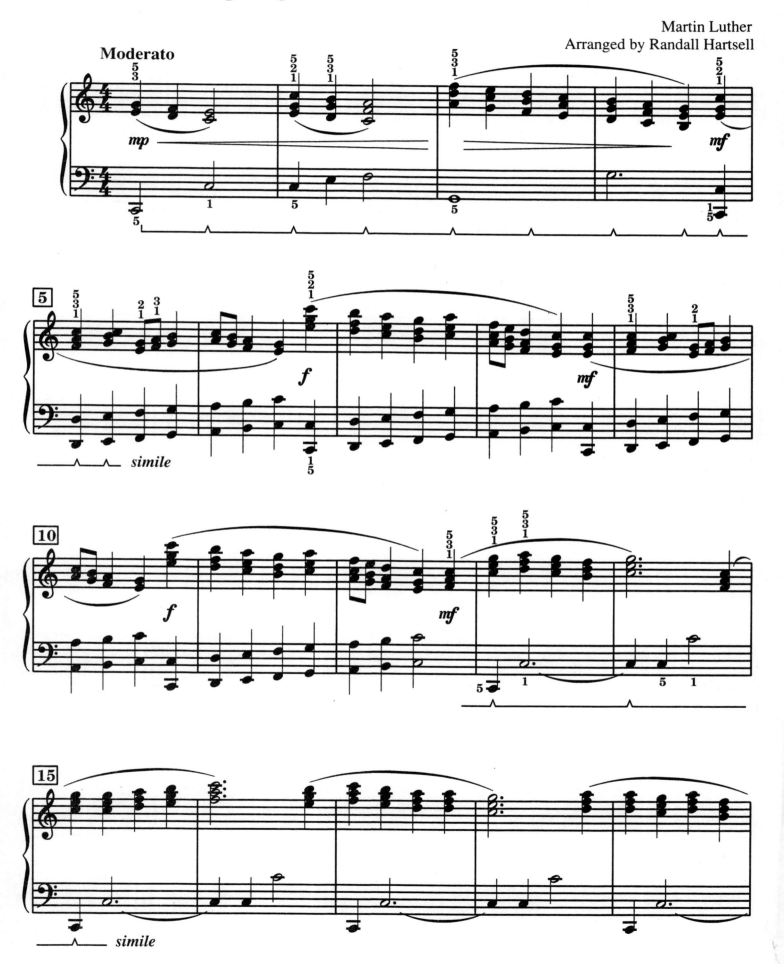

Holy, Holy, Holy

John B. Dykes
Arranged by Randall Hartsell

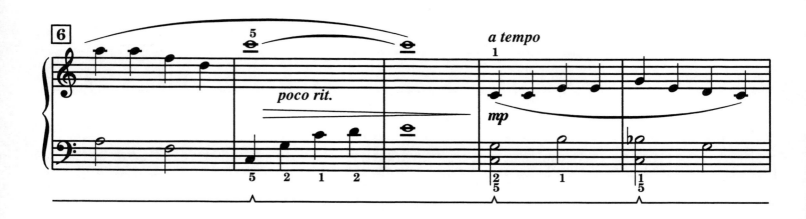

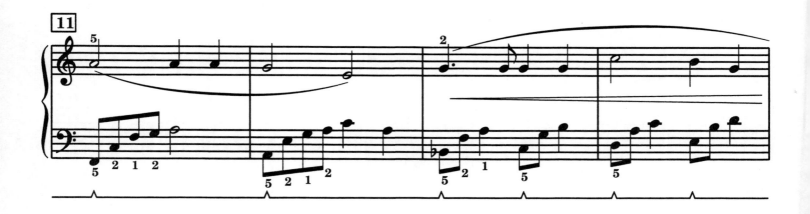

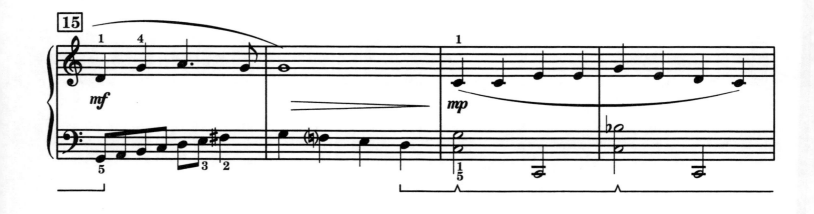

Jesus, the Very Thought of You

John B. Dykes
Arranged by Randall Hartsell

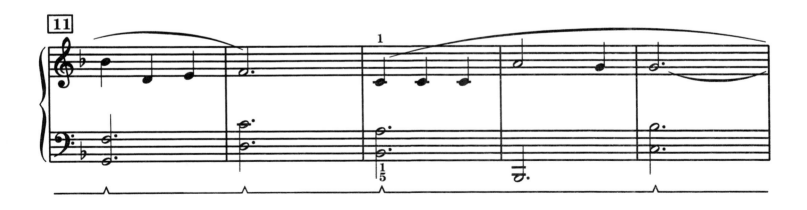

17

Kum Ba Ya

Spiritual
Arranged by Randall Hartsell

19

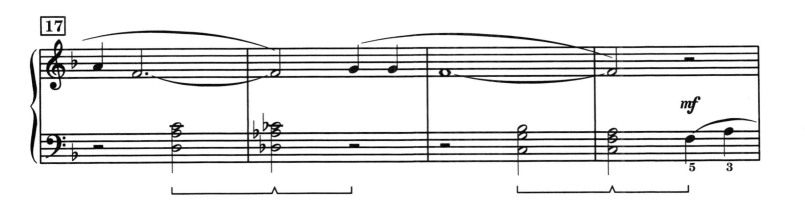

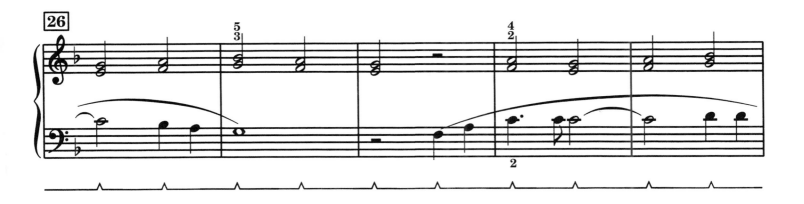

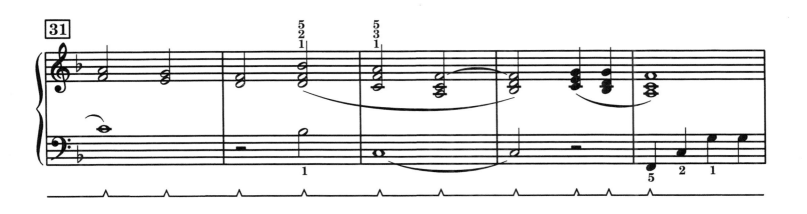